W9-DDN-636

THE
SAINT
BERNARD

by Charlotte Wilcox

Content Consultant:
Cheryl Zappala
Saint Bernard Club of America

C A P S T O N E   P R E S S
M A N K A T O ,   M I N N E S O T A

C A P S T O N E   P R E S S

818 North Willow Street • Mankato, MN 56001
www.capstone-press.com

Printed in the United States of America.

Library of Congress Cataloging-in-Publication Data
Wilcox, Charlotte.
    The Saint Bernard/by Charlotte Wilcox.
    p. cm.--(Learning about dogs)
    Includes bibliographical references and index.
    Summary: An introduction to a dog breed originating in Switzerland,
including its history, development, uses, and care.
    ISBN 1-56065-544-5
    1. Saint Bernard dog--Juvenile literature. [1. Saint Bernard dog.
2. Dogs.] I. Title. II. Series: Wilcox, Charlotte. Learning about dogs.
SF429.S3W55 1998
636.73--dc21

                                97-16363
                                  CIP
                                     AC

Photo credits
Archive Photos, 12, 22
Jean S. Buldain, 34, 28, 30
Bob Firth, 18, 38
Int'l Stock Photo, 17
Reynolds Photography, cover, 14, 25, 26, 36
David Sailors, 10
Lynn M. Stone, 6
Unicorn/Jim Shippee, 8; Deborah L. Martin, 32
Faith A. Uridel, 4, 20, 40-41

Table of Contents

Quick Facts about the Saint Bernard

Description

Height: Male Saint Bernards stand 27-1/2 to 35-1/2 inches (70 to 90 centimeters) tall. Females stand 25-1/2 to 31-1/2 inches (65 to 80 centimeters) tall. The height is measured from the ground to the withers. The withers are the tops of the shoulders.

Weight: Most Saint Bernards weigh from 120 to 200 pounds (54 to 90 kilograms). Males usually weigh more than females.

Physical features:	The Saint Bernard is a heavyweight dog. It has a large head with droopy ears. Its eyes and mouth are also droopy. Its tail is long and bushy.
Color:	Saint Bernards are white with patches of reddish or golden brown or brindle. Brindle is many shades of brown.

Development

Place of origin:	Saint Bernards were developed in Switzerland.
History of breed:	Saint Bernards came from Swiss farm dogs.
Numbers:	About 6,500 Saint Bernards are registered every year in the United States. Almost 500 are registered each year in Canada. Register means to record a dog's breeding record with an official club.

Uses

Most Saint Bernards in North America are family pets. They can be trained to pull carts or sleds. In Switzerland, some are still farm dogs.

Chapter 1

Saints and Guardian Angels

The Saint Bernard is named for the Great Saint Bernard Pass in Switzerland. This place is high in the Alps mountains on the border between Switzerland and Italy. One of the few roads between Switzerland and Italy goes through this pass. Weather there is fierce in the winter.

A Roman Catholic monk built a monastery in the Great Saint Bernard Pass about 1,000 years ago. A monk is a man who dedicates his life to serving a religious community. A monastery is a place where monks live.

The Saint Bernard is named for the Great Saint Bernard Pass in Switzerland.

Monasteries are often located in out-of-the-way places.

The monk who built the monastery in the pass was called Saint Bernard of Menthon. The pass and the monastery both came to be known by his name. Later, monks built an inn at the monastery. They provided food and shelter there for travelers.

Some of the monks became mountain guides. They led travelers through the mountains. The monks found their best helpers in local farm dogs. These dogs could find their way through a blizzard or heavy fog. They could find a person buried under piles of snow.

By the early 1700s, the monks were breeding these dogs on their monastery grounds. The dogs became famous for rescuing travelers lost in the snow. They later came to be known as the Saint Bernard dogs.

Saint Bernards were famous for rescuing lost travelers in the snow.

Chapter 2

The Beginnings of the Breed

No one knows when large dogs with red and white patches first appeared in Switzerland. They were part of farm life there for many centuries. They herded cattle and sheep. They carried supplies on their backs. They guarded the farms from wolves and robbers. They played with farmers' children.

The monks of the Great Saint Bernard Pass chose these farm dogs as helpers. They first began using the dogs around the year 1700. The monks became expert dog breeders. They raised dogs that were strong and dependable.

Many breeds came from the mastiff. The mastiff is an ancient breed of large dogs. Some

Monks began using Saint Bernards around the year 1700.

of the oldest are the Irish wolfhound and the English mastiff. These breeds were well known in Europe more than 1,000 years ago.

The Monks' Dogs

These first dogs had short coats. Some winters were harsh, and several dogs died on rescue missions. The monks decided to bring in some Newfoundlands to breed with their dogs.

Newfoundlands have long, thick coats. The monks thought this would help their dogs endure severe weather. But they were wrong. The snow stuck in the dogs' long hair when they had to travel far through deep snow. The dogs became so weighted down with snow and ice that they could not move.

The monks stopped using long-haired dogs for breeding. They gave away all the puppies born with long hair. But people in the nearby farms and towns liked the long-haired dogs. They bred them with other dogs from the region. Since then, Saint Bernards have been born with either short or long coats.

The monks bred dogs that could withstand harsh winters.

Saint Bernards helped rescue about 2,000 travelers in the 1700s and 1800s.

Mountain Heroes

The monks and their dogs worked together in the pass for about 200 years. They rescued about 2,000 travelers during the 1700s and 1800s.

Between 1790 and 1810, hundreds of thousands of soldiers marched through the pass. The records from their armies show that no soldiers died in the pass. Many became lost, but all were rescued by the monks and their dogs.

The dogs and monks usually went on rescue missions together. But some groups of dogs were able to find and rescue people without the monks. When the dogs found someone in the snow, they would lie down next to the person. The heat from their bodies kept the person from freezing to death.

If the traveler was unconscious, the dogs would lick the person's face. Their licks woke the person. One of the dogs would rush home to the monastery. This dog would guide the monks back to the lost traveler.

Barry

One heroic Saint Bernard was born at the monastery in 1800. His name was Barry. He saved 40 lives during his service as a rescue dog.

After Barry died, people told stories about his heroic deeds. Someone built a monument to him in Paris, France. It says, "He saved the lives of 40 persons. He was killed by the 41st."

The words on the monument are not true. When Barry was 12 years old, he moved with one of the monks to Berne, Switzerland. Barry died in Berne in 1814.

The last dog rescue in the monastery records took place in 1897. Soon after that, people began traveling through the mountains in cars and trains. They no longer became stranded in the pass.

The monastery still stands in the Great Saint Bernard Pass. The monks still raise their famous dogs. They still honor the memory of Barry. They always keep one dog named Barry at the monastery.

The body of the original Barry was preserved. It is on display at Switzerland's Natural History Museum. Barry represents all the heroic dogs from the monastery in the Great Saint Bernard Pass.

The monks always keep one dog named Barry at the monastery.

Chapter 3

Development of the Saint Bernard

In the late 1800s, dog breeding was a popular hobby in Europe. Breeders from all over Europe admired the dogs from the monastery. Several breeders bought dogs from the monks. But the monks still needed the dogs. They would not sell many.

Some early Saint Bernard breeders also bought farm dogs from the area around the monastery. These dogs were much like the monks' dogs.

Heinrich Schumacher

The first breeder to keep a record of Saint Bernard births was Heinrich Schumacher. He lived near Berne. He owned a prize Saint Bernard named Barry I. This dog was born in

In the late 1800s, dog breeders from all over Europe admired the monks' Saint Bernards.

1854. Barry I was a grandson of dogs from the monastery.

Barry I was white with reddish-brown patches. He had a short coat. Schumacher bred him with a long-haired female named Blässi. She was from the monastery.

Schumacher raised many more puppies descended from Barry I and Blässi. He sold dogs to England, Russia, and the United States. Many modern Saint Bernards come from Barry I and Blässi.

Saint Bernards in the United States

In the mid-1800s, an American actor brought a large English dog on stage. People thought the dog was a Saint Bernard. It looked like a Saint Bernard, but it was not a real one. Many people sent for dogs like the actor's dog.

The true Saint Bernard breed did not come to the United States until later. Good breeding dogs were introduced in the United States, and the breed flourished.

Many modern Saint Bernards are descended from Barry I and Blässi.

Chapter 4

The Saint Bernard Today

The American Kennel Club registered its first Saint Bernard in 1885. The Saint Bernard Club of America began in 1888. Now, the American Kennel Club registers about 6,500 Saint Bernards every year. The Canadian Kennel Club registers almost 500 per year.

The Sizable Saint Bernard

The Saint Bernard is the heaviest dog breed recognized by the American Kennel Club. Saint Bernards are heavier and stronger than a grown man. They have large heads with

The American Kennel Club registers about 6,500 Saint Bernards every year.

powerful jaws. They have droopy mouths, eyes, and ears. These features give Saint Bernards a quiet, gentle appearance.

Saint Bernard puppies weigh about one and one-half pounds (less than one kilogram) at birth. During the first year, they add about three pounds (nearly one and one-half kilograms) each week. Puppies grow to 100 times their birth weight in three years.

When fully grown, Saint Bernards usually weigh between 120 and 200 pounds (54 to 90 kilograms). Males are usually heavier than females. The largest Saint Bernard on record weighed 310 pounds (140 kilograms).

Adult males average 27-1/2 to 35-1/2 inches (70 to 90 centimeters) tall. Females stand 25-1/2 to 31-1/2 inches (65 to 80 centimeters) tall. Height is measured from the ground to the withers. The withers are the tops of the shoulders.

Saint Bernards have droopy mouths, eyes, and ears.

Colors and Coat Types

A Saint Bernard is white on its chest, neck, feet, the bridge of its nose, and the tip of its tail. It has patches of tan or brown. The patches can be any color from light golden brown to deep reddish brown. Some Saint Bernards have brindle-colored patches. Brindle is many shades of brown. Many Saint Bernards have dark shadings on the head and ears. Some have a white stripe called a blaze on their faces.

Saint Bernards can be short-haired or long-haired. The color patterns are the same for both coat types. The short coats are smooth and very thick. Long coats may be slightly wavy. Long-haired Saint Bernards have shorter hair on their heads. Both types have bushy hair on the thighs and tail.

Some Saint Bernards have a white stripe called a blaze on their faces.

Chapter 5

Rescue Stories

People tell stories about Saint Bernard rescues. One of the first Saint Bernards to earn the Dog Hero of the Year award was named Beggar. He pulled a three-year-old boy out of a flooded river in California. He earned the award in 1962.

Grizzly Bear

Another dog hero was named Grizzly Bear. He was from Alaska. One day, Grizzly Bear's owner was attacked by a real grizzly. The owner accidentally walked between the female bear and its cub.

The owner fainted when the bear grabbed her arm. Her Saint Bernard attacked the bear fearlessly. He scared the bear into the woods. Both the owner and her dog walked away without serious injury.

People tell stories about Saint Bernard rescues.

Budweiser

Members of a South Carolina family owe their lives to a Saint Bernard named Budweiser. Budweiser spent his early life tied up in someone's yard. He was lonely and hard to control. But he found a loving home when he was given to an elderly couple.

Budweiser was one year old when he went to live with the couple. One evening, the couple's small grandchildren stayed overnight. Just as the children were going to bed, there was a huge explosion in the house.

Everything was on fire in an instant. Budweiser was on the front porch. He rushed into the children's burning bedroom. Budweiser grabbed the smallest girl by her shirt. He dragged her out of the house and onto a neighbor's doorstep.

Budweiser ran back into the house. He pulled another girl to safety. By this time, all the people were out of the house. Budweiser went back for the family's other dog. It was a tiny Chihuahua. But the flames were too strong. Budweiser had to turn back.

Budweiser's paws were burned. His lungs were hurt by smoke. But none of the children or their grandparents were injured.

Many people owe their lives to Saint Bernards.

Chapter 6

Owning a Saint Bernard

Most Saint Bernards never have to rescue anyone. But Saint Bernards are sometimes called baby-sitter dogs. They seem to understand children in a special way. They are not always aware of their own size. One wag of a Saint Bernard's tail can knock a child over.

Saint Bernards seldom bark without a good reason. They will alert the family when a visitor or stranger arrives. But they are too friendly to be serious guard dogs.

Saint Bernards do not have a long life span. They usually live to be seven to 12 years old. This is typical of many large dog breeds.

Saint Bernards are sometimes called baby-sitter dogs.

Keeping a Saint Bernard

Saint Bernards are calm and quiet. They do not romp or run around much. A long walk every day is about all the exercise they need.

Saint Bernards are seldom wild and noisy, but obedience training is still needed. Obedience is obeying rules and commands. Puppies should start obedience classes when they are about six months old. A good training program lasts two or three months.

Many people have their names and phone numbers put on their dogs' collars. Some owners have a microchip implanted under the dog's skin. A microchip is a computer chip about the size of a grain of rice. When scanned, it reveals the owner's name, address, and telephone number.

Feeding a Saint Bernard

Saint Bernards eat plenty of food. But they do not eat as much as large breeds that are more active. A full-grown Saint Bernard may eat

Saint Bernards are calm and quiet.

two pounds (one kilogram) of dog food every day. It is best to divide the food into at least two meals.

Saint Bernards should always have clean water. If this is not possible, Saint Bernards must be able to drink at least three times a day.

Grooming

Saint Bernards shed much of their hair during the spring and fall. They can also shed during the rest of the year. A weekly brushing is needed to keep the Saint Bernard's coat in good shape.

Saint Bernards should not have a bath more than once or twice a year. Bathing can make their shedding worse. Saint Bernards often drool. An owner should be prepared to clean up after a drooling dog.

Other grooming needs include trimming the dog's toenails and cleaning its teeth. Its ears should be cleaned once a month. A veterinarian can show a dog owner how to do these things.

Saint Bernards shed much of their hair during the spring and fall.

People looking for Saint Bernard puppies should contact a Saint Bernard club.

A veterinarian is a person trained and qualified to treat the sicknesses and injuries of animals.

Health Care

Dogs need shots every year to protect them from serious sicknesses. They need pills to protect them from heartworms.

A heartworm is a tiny worm carried by mosquitoes that enters a dog's heart and slowly destroys it. Dogs also need a checkup every year for all types of worms.

Dogs should be checked for ticks every day during warm weather. A tick is a small bug that sucks blood. Some ticks carry Lyme disease. Lyme disease is a serious illness that can cripple an animal or a human. Dogs should also be checked all year for fleas, lice, and mites. These are tiny insects that live on a dog's skin.

Searching for a Saint Bernard

People looking for Saint Bernard puppies should contact a Saint Bernard club. The club can recommend a good breeder. A rescue shelter can help locate a grown Saint Bernard. Rescue shelters find homes for abandoned dogs. A dog from a shelter usually costs less than one from a breeder. Some dogs in shelters are even free. Many are already trained.

Hindquarters

Hock

Withers

Ears

Muzzle

Shoulder

Forequarters

Quick Facts about Dogs

Dog Terms

A male dog is called a dog. A female dog is known as a bitch. A young dog is a puppy until it is one year old. A newborn puppy is a whelp until it no longer depends on its mother's milk. A family of puppies born at one time is called a litter.

Life History

Origin:
: All dogs, wolves, coyotes, and dingoes descended from a single wolflike species. Dogs have been friends of humans since earliest times.

Types:
: There are many colors, shapes, and sizes of dogs. Full-grown dogs weigh from two pounds (one kilogram) to more than 200 pounds (90 kilograms). They are from six inches (15 centimeters) to three feet (90 centimeters) tall. They can have thick hair or almost no hair, long or short legs, and many types of ears, faces, and tails. There are about 350 different dog breeds in the world.

Reproductive life:
: Dogs mature at six to 18 months. Puppies are born two months after breeding. A female can have two litters per year. An average litter is three to six puppies, but litters of 15 or more are possible.

Development:
: Puppies are born blind and deaf. Their ears and eyes open at one to two weeks. They try to walk at about two weeks. At three weeks, their teeth begin to come in.

| Life span: | Dogs are fully grown at two years. If well cared for, they may live up to 15 years. |

The Dog's Super Senses

Smell:	Dogs have a sense of smell many times stronger than a human's. Dogs use their sensitive noses even more than their eyes and ears. They recognize people, animals, and objects just by smelling them. Sometimes they recognize them from long distances or for days afterward.
Hearing:	Dogs hear better than humans. Not only can dogs hear things from farther away, they can hear high-pitched sounds people cannot.
Sight:	Dogs are probably color-blind. Some scientists think dogs can see some colors. Others think dogs see everything in black and white. Dogs can see twice as wide around them as humans can because their eyes are on the sides of their heads.
Touch:	Dogs enjoy being petted more than almost any other animal. They can feel vibrations like an approaching train or an earthquake about to happen.
Taste:	Dogs do not taste much. This is partly because their sense of smell is so strong that it overpowers their taste. It is also because they swallow their food too quickly to taste it well.
Navigation:	Dogs can often find their way through crowded streets or across miles of wilderness without any guidance. This is a special dog ability that scientists do not fully understand.

Words to Know

blaze (BLAYZ)—a white stripe down the middle of an animal's face

brindle (BRIN-duhl)—streaked shades of brown

heartworm (HART-wurm)—a tiny worm carried by mosquitoes that enters a dog's heart and slowly destroys it

Lyme disease (LIME duh-ZEEZ)—a disease carried by ticks that can cripple an animal or a human

monastery (MON-uh-ster-ee)—a place where monks live

monk (MUHNGK)—a man who dedicates his life to serving a religious community

obedience (oh-BEE-dee-uhnss)—obeying rules and commands

register (REJ-uh-stur)—to record a dog's breeding records with an official club

veterinarian (vet-ur-uh-NER-ee-uhn)—a person trained and qualified to treat the sicknesses and injuries of animals

wean (WEEN)—to stop depending on a mother's milk

withers (WITH-urs)—the tops of an animal's shoulders

To Learn More

Alderton, David. *Dogs*. New York: Dorling Kindersley, 1993.

American Kennel Club. *The Complete Dog Book.* New York: Macmillan Publishing Co., 1992.

Muggleton, Pat, Michael Wensley and Ann Wensley. *The Complete Saint Bernard.* New York: Howell Book House, 1992.

Tine, Robert. *Beethoven's Puppies.* Panama City, Fla.: Boulevard Books, 1996.

Weil, Martin. *Saint Bernards.* Neptune City, N.J.: T.F.H. Publications, 1982.

Wood, Gerald L. *The Guinness Book of Pet Records.* Enfield, Middlesex, Great Britain: Guinness Superlatives, 1984.

You can read articles about Saint Bernards in *AKC Gazette, Dog Fancy, Dog World,* and *The Saint Fancier* magazines.

Useful Addresses

American Kennel Club
5580 Centerview Drive
Raleigh, NC 27606

Canadian Kennel Club
100-89 Skyway Avenue
Etobicoke, ON M9W 6R4
Canada

Natural History Museum
Bernastrasse 15
CH-3005 Berne
Switzerland

Saint Bernard Club of America
1043 South 140th Street
Seattle, WA 98168

Internet Sites

Acme Pet
http://www.acmepet.com

Welcome to the AKC
http://www.akc.org

Natural History Museum Berne Switzerland
http://www-nmbe.unibe.ch/

Welcome to k9web
http://www.k9Web.com

Index